D1544992

STICKY FINGERS

GROWING THINGS

by Ting and Neil Morris

Illustrated by
Ruth Levy

FRANKLIN WATTS

NEW YORK/CHICAGO/LONDON/TORONTO/SYDNEY

This symbol appears on some pages throughout this book. It indicates that adult supervision is advisable for that activity.

© Franklin Watts 1994

Franklin Watts

10 9 8 7 6 5 4 3 2

Library of Congress Cataloging-in-Publication Data

Morris, Ting.
Growing Things/by Ting and Neil Morris
p. cm. -- (Sticky Fingers)
Includes bibliographical references and index
ISBN 0-531-14284-1
1. Gardening--Juvenile Literature.
2. Plant propagation--Juvenile Literature.
3. Container gardening--Juvenile Literature. 4. Growth (Plants) --
Experiments--Juvenile Literature (1. Gardening. 2. Container gardening.
3. Growth (Plants)--Experiments. 4. Experiments) I. Morris, Neil. II Title.
III. Series: Morris, Ting. Sticky Fingers.
SB457.M67 1994
635.9'86--dc20   93-41957
                                        CIP AC

Editor: Hazel Poole
Designer: Sally Boothroyd
Photography: John Butcher
Artwork: Ruth Levy
Picture research: Juliet Duff

Printed in Malaysia

All rights reserved

Contents

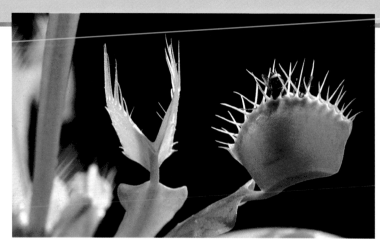

Introduction

In this book you can learn something about growing things both by reading about plants and by having fun with simple gardening activities. The information in the fact boxes will tell you about different plants – where they come from, how they grow, and how the seasons affect them. You will also learn something about seeds, bulbs, and buds, as well as how plants use sunlight and how some even catch insects!

At the end of the book there is information on the parts of a plant and flower, and on how to plant seeds. There is also a list of books to read if you want to find out more.

Now you can get ready to get your fingers muddy and sticky – growing things as you read about plants.

Equipment, materials, and plants

The projects in this book show you how to grow plants and take care of them. You won't need much adult help or a large plot of land to make a garden in pots, boxes, and jars. Old kitchen knives, forks, scissors, and a water spray bottle make useful indoor gardening tools. A trowel and a watering can are needed for big planting activities. You can grow plants in any container that holds enough earth for the roots to develop and has drainage holes in the bottom. Ordinary soil can be used for growing plants, but special potting compost gives the best results. Compost, seeds, bulbs, and plants can be bought in plant stores or garden centers. Before you start on an activity, gather all the things you will need. Follow the instructions carefully, and your windowsill will soon turn into a growing success story!

The following items are used in this book:

apple
banana seeds
blotting paper
bread (white)
broad bean seeds
brush
bulb jar (optional)
cacti
cactus compost
canes (small garden stakes)
carnivorous plant compost
charcoal (optional)
cheese
cling wrap
containers (various sizes)
cress seeds
daffodil bulbs
flowerpots
food tray
forsythia twigs
gardening gloves
glass bowl (shallow)
gravel

haricot bean seeds
horse chestnut twigs
hyacinth bulbs
ice-cream container
jam
jars
knife
labels
magnifying glass
margarine tub
measuring cup
newspaper
notepad
paint (enamel)
paper towels
pear twigs
pebbles
pencil
petals
pitcher plant or Venus's-
    flytrap
plastic bags (clear)

potato
potting compost
radish
rainwater
runner bean seeds
saucer
shells
soap
soil
sticks
stones
string
thermos
toothpicks
twigs
water
water lilies (miniature)
wood
yogurt cup

Budding Branches

Here's how to have a touch of spring in the middle of winter.

YOU WILL NEED:
- leafless forsythia, pear, and horse chestnut twigs
- 3 jars   ✓ 3 labels
- notepad and pencil
- water

1 Take a look at trees and bushes during the winter months. Most of them have no leaves, but their branches have plenty of tiny buds, waiting for the warm spring sunshine. Ask an adult to help you cut twigs from a forsythia bush, pear tree, and horse chestnut.

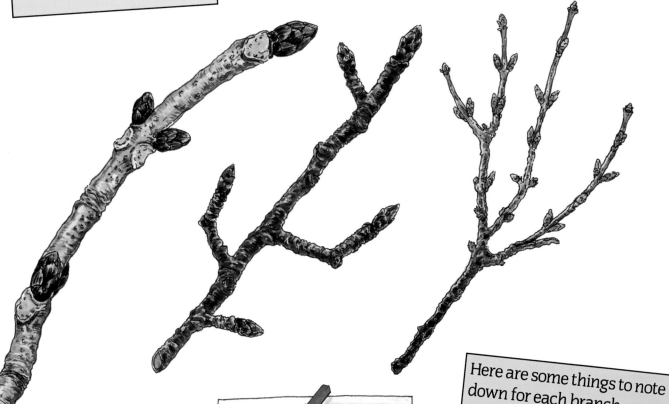

2 Put each twig in its own jar of water. Label the jars with the name of the plant from which the twig came.

Here are some things to note down for each branch:
date of cutting
length of twig and size of bud
room temperature
date of: scales falling off buds
buds unfolding
leaves unfurling
leaves opening out
flowering

3 Keep a chart for each twig, noting down everything you see. Draw each changing stage, and don't forget to add the date to all your drawings and notes. Then you can compare the progress of your budding branches.

Buds

Buds contain leaves and flowers that are folded and pressed together in a neat, tight package. The outside of the package is usually covered with scales, which protect the bud and keep it dry. When the spring brings warmer weather, the scales fall off and the bud slowly unfolds. The buds that open in spring start to grow almost a year earlier, but they are so small that we hardly notice them. Most of the buds along the sides of a branch are leaf buds. There are separate buds for flowers, but some trees wrap their leaves and flowers in the same package. The yellow bell-shaped flowers of the forsythia shrub come out before the leaves. The horse chestnut tree has sticky brown leaf buds. Some types of bee use this sticky coating as a glue to patch up their hives. The horse chestnut produces prickly green fruits that contain shiny brown seeds, which are sometimes called buckeyes.

Which budding branch is your favorite?

7

Full of Beans

It's easy to watch beans grow and climb.

YOU WILL NEED:
- ✔ *yogurt cup* ✔ *large jam jar* ✔ *paper towels*
- ✔ *6 runner bean, broad bean or haricot bean seeds* ✔ *bucket-sized flowerpot* ✔ *string*
- ✔ *small stones* ✔ *potting compost* ✔ *water*
- ✔ *3 long garden canes or stakes*

1 Put a yogurt cup upside down in a large jam jar. Then roll four sheets of paper towel into a tube and push this into the jar and around the pot. Wet the paper thoroughly.

2 Push the dried beans between the glass and the paper, so that they stay there without falling to the bottom. Pour some water into the jar to keep the paper wet. Then stand the jar in a warm, sunny place.

3 Make sure that the paper is kept damp, and you can watch the beans grow. The skin of each bean swells, splits, and sprouts. You will soon see roots growing downward and shoots growing upward.

4 Once your bean plants produce leaves, they will grow very fast. When the shoots are about 6 inches (15 cm) long, transplant them into a large flowerpot. First put some stones over the holes in the bottom of the pot, and then fill it with potting compost. Build a climbing frame for your beans by sticking three garden canes into the pot. Tie the canes together at the top.

5 Make small holes in the compost next to the canes, and put a bean plant in each hole. Cover the roots with compost, and then give the flowerpot a good watering. Keep the plant on a balcony or patio.

6 Always keep the compost damp. As the plants grow, wind them around the canes.

7 When little red flowers appear on the plants, spray them with water to help the pods grow.

8 When the pods are about 4 inches (10 cm) long, you can pick them and enjoy your very own bean feast!

Beans

Beans are the seeds of pod-bearing plants. Each bean is covered by a hard seed coat, which protects the embryo seedling inside. The bean contains a store of food that is used up as the seedling grows. One part of the embryo is a very short stem that produces a root at its lower end. The upper part of the embryo is a bud with two tiny leaves. This grows into the stem and leaves of the bean plant. In order to sprout, beans need warmth, moisture, and air. Given these conditions, the stored food passes to the growing regions of the embryo. The embryo bursts through the seed coat and emerges as a young plant that begins to look like its bean parent. The food stored inside a bean includes protein. Humans and animals also need protein to grow, and that is one reason why we eat beans. With runner beans or kidney beans, you eat the pods too.

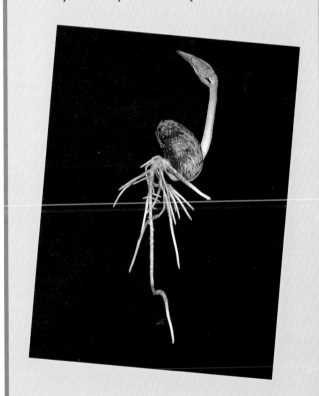

Miniature Japanese Lake

YOU WILL NEED:
✔ large shallow glass bowl ✔ soil ✔ gravel
✔ pebbles ✔ 1 miniature water lily ✔ twig
✔ shells ✔ measuring cup ✔ water
✔ petals, leaves

1 First fill the bottom of a shallow glass bowl to a depth of 1 inch (3 cm) with ordinary soil. Then cover the soil with a thin layer of gravel.

2 Collect some pebbles and shells, looking out for interesting or unusual shapes and colors. Arrange these on the gravel base. Push a small twig through the gravel into the soil. Try to make your arrangement look simple.

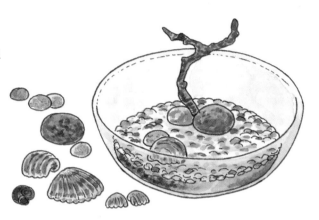

3 Use a measuring cup to half-fill the bowl with water. Then decorate the surface with leaves and petals, to look like water lilies in bloom.

4 You could grow a real lily in your lake. In late spring you can buy miniature water lilies from an aquarium store or garden center. To plant the lily, scoop out the water and put the plant in the gravel and soil. Then pour enough water into the bowl to cover the lily. Keep adding water to the pond as the lily grows.

Flower arranging

The beautiful art of flower arranging is called *ikebana* in Japanese. This art started in ancient China, where Buddhist monks decorated their temples with flowers. When Buddhism was introduced to Japan in the sixth century, Japanese monks carried on the tradition. Over the centuries, flower arrangements became popular with Japanese lords and warriors. Today *ikebana* is still taught in special schools. Arrangements can show the change of seasons, or the growth of a plant from bud to blossom. Others have miniature ponds or show country scenes. The charm of these arrangements lies in their simple beauty. Each flower is arranged so that it stands out in a plain bowl or vase, and the container is never crowded. Traditional arrangements are based on three lines. The longest line stands for Heaven, the second line for man, and the third line for earth. The arrangement may be made up only of flowers, or branches and leaves may be used too.

Isn't your lake simply beautiful?

Banana Plant

Growing a banana plant needs lots of patience and a little bit of luck.

YOU WILL NEED:
- ✔ banana seeds   ✔ small container
- ✔ potting compost   ✔ clear plastic bag or wrap   ✔ thermos (optional)   ✔ water
- ✔ 3-inch (8-cm) and larger flowerpots

1 You can buy banana seeds in most garden centers. Some also sell complete kits for growing your own bananas. If you get a kit, follow the instructions on the package. If you have seeds, soak them for two days in warm water before planting. You could put them in a thermos, so that the water temperature stays about the same.

2 Fill a small container with potting compost. Sow the banana seeds $1/2$ inch (1 cm) deep in the compost, and then water so that the compost is moist.

3 Cover the container with clear plastic, and put it in a warm place. The seeds need a constant temperature of about 68°F (20°C) to germinate. Don't put the container in strong sunlight – a warm windowsill or cupboard is best. Check regularly to make sure that the compost is moist – not soaking wet – and water when necessary.

4 It will take 8 to 10 weeks for the first seedlings to appear. When they do, take the plastic off and put the container in a warm, light place.

5 When the plants are about $1 1/2$ inches (4 cm) high, transplant them into bigger pots. Now they will grow very quickly. Make sure the compost is moist, and keep the pots in good light at a temperature of at least 65°F (18°C).

6 As the plants grow, transplant them into even bigger pots. If you are lucky, your banana plant might grow as tall as 7 feet (2 m) in three months. If you are very lucky, you might even get bananas.

Tropical plants

Many different delicious fruits grow in the tropical regions of the world. Bananas and pineapples are probably the most popular tropical fruits. The banana plant is often called a tree, but there is no wood in its stem. The plant's stem is actually the bases of its leaves growing one inside the other. The big leaves that spread out at the top of the stem are sometimes more than 10 feet (3 m) long. The plant is between 10 and 30 feet (3 and 9m) tall when it is old enough to produce fruit. The bananas grow in bunches. Each bunch has 5 to 16 clusters of fruit, called "hands," and each hand has 10 to 20 separate bananas, sometimes called "fingers." When they first appear, the small bananas point downward, but as they grow bigger they turn and point upward. This makes them look as if they are growing upside down! In three or four months they are ready to be picked. After each banana plant produces one bunch of fruit it dies and its stem is removed. A new stem grows in its place and other plants grow beside it from the underground stem to produce more bananas.

Not all banana seeds are successful. Unlucky growers should not go bananas, but try again!

Getting Moldy

You don't need green fingers to grow fungus!

YOU WILL NEED:
✓ slice of white bread   ✓ cheese   ✓ 3 clear plastic bags
✓ 3 teaspoons jam   ✓ small jar   ✓ cling wrap   ✓ apple
✓ notepad and pencil   ✓ magnifying glass

1 Put half an apple in one plastic bag, a slice of white bread in another, and a chunk of cheese – cheddar grows a good crop – in the third. Then put a few teaspoons of jam into a small jar and seal the top with cling wrap.

2 Put the plastic bags and the jar in a warm place, and wait for the mold to grow.

3 Check your mold plantation after three days. From then on keep a record of what happens to each mold. Use a magnifying glass to note size, shape, and colors. Draw what you see.

4 Check again after another seven days. But don't open the bags – an unpleasant smell comes with the furry growth! By now you will be able to see a network of tiny tubes. These break the food down into a liquid. You may also see small stalks with capsules at the top. The capsules contain spores, which would float away to create mold somewhere else. This is another reason for not opening the bag and releasing the spores into the air.

5 After two or three weeks you should have a good mold collection and an interesting growth record. If there is a compost heap in your garden, you could put the mold onto it. Fungi help to break down the dead material that provides nutrients for the garden. Otherwise, put the mold bags and jar in the trash can.

Be very careful *never* to touch or eat mold.

Fungi

Mushrooms are the best-known fungi, but there are over 100,000 different kinds of fungi (the plural of fungus). Mold, mildew, and yeast are also fungi, and they are all very simple living things. Fungi have no roots, stems, leaves, seeds, or flowers. They cannot produce their own food, so must get nourishment from living things or from material that was once part of a plant or an animal. This material might be rotten wood, bread, fruit, or cheese. Unlike green plants, fungi can live in the dark. The best time to look for them is when it is mild and damp, usually in late autumn. In the woods you can find mushrooms in the dead leaves around trees and among piles of old logs. But you must *never* touch or eat any fungi that you may find: there are more than 70 different kinds of poisonous mushrooms! Some people use the name "mushroom" for fungi that can be eaten, and call poisonous fungi "toadstools."

Bulb Presents

You can make a blooming Christmas present by planting bulbs in the autumn to flower in midwinter. Bulbs can be "forced," or hurried, if they are planted indoors about four months before you want them to flower.

YOU WILL NEED:
✔ *large shallow flowerpot (optional)* ✔ *potting compost*
✔ *ice-cream or margarine tub* ✔ *enamel paint and brush*
✔ *gravel or small pebbles* ✔ *bulb jar (optional)* ✔ *sticks*
✔ *hyacinth and daffodil bulbs* ✔ *string* ✔ *yogurt cup*
✔ *jelly jar* ✔ *water*

1 Use a big shallow flowerpot for planting, or you could make your own bulb bowl. Ask an adult to pierce small drainage holes in the bottom of an ice-cream or margarine tub. Then decorate the tub with a painted pattern. You could include the name of the person who is to receive the present. Wait for the paint to dry before using the bowl for planting.

2 Put some gravel or a few small pebbles at the bottom of the bowl. Cover these with a layer of potting compost.

3 Place three daffodil bulbs on the compost, pointed end up. Put compost on top of the bulbs, and press it down firmly. As a rule, small bulbs must be completely covered, but big bulbs, such as daffodils and tulips, can stick out of the compost slightly. Water the bulbs – the compost should be moist but not soaking wet.

4 Put the bowl in a cool, dark place such as a shed or a cold cupboard. Check the compost regularly to make sure that it is damp.

5 After about 8 to 10 weeks, when the leaves are about 1¹/₂ inches (4 cm) high, move the bowl to a cool windowsill. Keep watering so the compost is always moist.

6 Soon the leaves will have grown to about 4 inches (10 cm) high, and it is time to move the plants to a warmer spot. Push sticks into the compost and use string to support tall flowers. Now your bowl of flowers is ready to give away. Don't forget to remind your friend to water their present!

Bulbs

A bulb is an underground storage organ for certain plants. It looks rather like an onion, and in fact a real onion is the bulb of the onion plant. Bulbs are made up of the bases of many thick, overlapping leaves. At the center of the leaves is a tiny bud. Food stored in the leaves nourishes the bud, and in time the bud sprouts. Roots grow from the bottom of the bulb to feed it water through the growing and flowering period. Leaves should be left on the plant after the flower has died, until they are yellow and dry and can be plucked off easily. They will then have had enough time to feed the bulb for next year's growth.

7 You could also grow a hyacinth in water. Use a special bulb jar, or make your own by cutting the bottom out of a yogurt cup and fitting it into a jelly jar. Fill the jar with water so that it covers the bottom of the bulb. Keep the jar in a dark place until the roots are 4 inches (10 cm) long. Then move it to a light place and watch your hyacinth bloom.

Insect-eaters

Garden centers usually have a selection of insectivorous plants and seedlings, such as the pitcher plant and Venus's-flytrap. Spring is the best time for growing them. In autumn and winter they take a rest from catching insects, and their leaves wither. This activity is not for the squeamish!

YOU WILL NEED:
✔ plant (optional) or seedling of pitcher plant or Venus's-flytrap   ✔ 3-in (8-cm) flowerpot
✔ rainwater   ✔ clear plastic bag   ✔ saucer
✔ carnivorous plant compost

1 If you buy a pitcher plant as a seedling, it will take three years before it is a fully grown insect-trapper. A Venus's-flytrap is ready to "hunt" in a year. Make sure you have collected as much rainwater as possible before you start.

2 Fill the bottom of the flowerpot with carnivorous plant compost. Plant your seedling, cover the roots, and water it well with rainwater. If it doesn't rain, use boiled and cooled tap water. Then stand the pot in a saucer filled with more rainwater.

3 Cover the pot with a clear plastic bag. Put the covered seedling in a warm, light place, but not in direct sunlight. Check that the soil stays moist.

4 After a week, make some holes in the bag to give your pitcher seedling more light and air. Then after another week, take the bag away and put the pot on a sunny windowsill. Make sure it always stands in a saucer half-filled with rainwater, and never water the plant from above. Soon your pitcher plant will be able to trap its own meals.

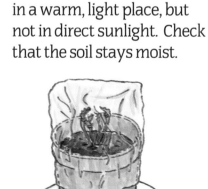

There is no need to force-feed insect-eaters with tiny pieces of meat or cheese.

Insectivorous plants

Insectivorous plants catch and feed on insects. The Venus's-flytrap is the best known of these amazing plants. It comes originally from the coastal regions of North and South Carolina. Its leaves are hinged in the middle, and the spiny edges mesh together. The leaves are usually partly open, showing a reddish surface inside. On that surface there are small sensitive hairs. When something touches two of the hairs, one after the other, the leaf closes and traps its prey – usually an insect. The leaf trap stays closed for about a week while plant fluids slowly dissolve the captured insect. Then it opens and waits for the next insect to come along.

Pitcher plants catch insects in a different way. They give off a sweet smell to lure prey into their tube-like leaves. The insect falls into a pool of liquid at the bottom of the "pitcher," and drowns. The liquid contains chemicals that digest it.

Insectivorous plants need less water in winter, when they are dormant. In winter keep your plant in a cool place and the soil damp. Next spring it will be back, hunting more insects!

Grow Your Own Name

...and put it in a sandwich.

YOU WILL NEED:
- ✔ *blotting paper or 2 layers of paper towel*
- ✔ *small food tray or dish* ✔ *pencil* ✔ *water*
- ✔ *2 packets of cress seeds*

1 Write your name on the paper in large capitals, leaving a good space between the letters. If your name is very long (Alexandra/Alexander), make sure you have a tray long enough to fit the paper – or shorten your name (Alex)! Fit the paper into a food tray or dish. Lazy writers can grow their initial (A).

2 Soak the paper with water. Then shake cress seeds onto the letter(s), pushing them close together with your fingers so that there are no gaps.

3 Put the tray on a windowsill, and make sure that the paper is always damp.

4 It will take about one week to 10 days for your name to be fully grown. It is best when it is about 2 inches (5 cm) tall and an even green in color.

5 Now that you have seen your name, it is time to eat it! Cut the cress off near the bottom of the stalks, and make yourself a lovely cress sandwich.

Green plants

Plant leaves are green because they contain chlorophyll, a green pigment. This substance is essential to the way in which plants feed themselves. When chlorophyll takes in sunlight, it gains in energy. This energy is then used by the plant to carry out chemical changes and make its own food. The plant takes water from the soil, through its roots, and a gas called carbon dioxide from the air, through its leaves. Then it uses the energy from sunlight to turn the water and gas into a sugary food, which is carried to all parts of the plant in liquid sap. This is why plants need sunlight. If they get no light, they lose their green color. The whole process is called photosynthesis, which means "putting together through light." During the process plants also give off oxygen, which is the gas that we breathe to live. So plants are essential to human life on earth.

Pot of Potatoes

Potatoes are grown in fields, because each seed potato needs a lot of space to develop into a new potato plant. But if you don't have a field, you can grow potatoes in a pot! Plant them in the spring.

YOU WILL NEED:
✔ 10-inch (25-cm) flowerpot
✔ stones ✔ potting compost
✔ newspaper ✔ water
✔ potato

1 Leave a potato to sprout – this will take a couple of weeks. Then put the sprouting potato in a warm, light place. When the shoots are about 3/4 inch (2 cm) long, the potato is ready to plant. Leave two shoots on one side of the potato, and rub off all the others.

2 Put a few stones in the bottom of the flowerpot, and half-fill it with potting compost. Make a hole for the potato to fit in, and plant it with the shoots pointing up. Cover the rest of the potato with compost, and then water it. Make sure that the compost stays damp while the shoots are growing.

3 After about four weeks, green shoots will poke through the soil. Add more compost and don't forget to water. Keep adding compost as the green shoots appear, until the pot is full.

4 Keep watering the potato plant as it grows leaves and then flowers. When the plant has finished flowering, you must stop watering it. Otherwise the new potatoes in the soil would rot. As the soil dries out, the plant will die. Now is the time to harvest your crop.

5 Put some newspaper on the floor and tip the pot out. Have you grown enough potatoes for supper?

Potatoes

The potato plant first grew in the region of the Andes mountain range, in South America. When the Spanish invaded South America in the middle of the sixteenth century, they found Indian people growing potatoes. The invaders took potatoes back to Europe, and by the end of the century they were common in Spain and Italy. English explorers also brought back potatoes around this time. It grew well in Ireland and became the country's main food. But between 1845 and 1847 a terrible blight, or plant disease, killed off the Irish potato crop. Around one million people died of starvation, and another million emigrated to the United States and other countries. In 450 years potatoes have spread throughout the world. They are still an important part of Ireland's farming produce, but today the world's biggest producers are Russia, Poland, the United States, and Canada.

Hanging Garden

YOU WILL NEED:
- ✔ ivy cutting ✔ young spider plant (chlorophytum)
- ✔ 2 small (2 in/5-cm) flowerpots ✔ scissors
- ✔ potting compost
- ✔ hanging basket ✔ hairpin

1 To make a hanging garden in your room, look for a healthy ivy and potted spider plant. Both like to hang from pots, and you can grow new plants from them.

2 The best time to take an ivy cutting is in spring or summer. Choose a young shoot about 6 in (15 cm) long and cut it off just below where a leaf grows from the stem.

3 Take off the lowest leaves. Fill a small pot with compost and plant the stem up to its leaves – about 2 in (5 cm) deep in the soil. Then water it. Your ivy will grow roots in a month if it is kept in a cool, light place and watered regularly. When you see that it is growing well, and getting new leaves, re-pot it in fresh soil in a bigger pot.

4 Spider plants grow babies at the end of long runners after flowering. Cut a baby spider off when its roots are about 1 in (2 cm) long.

5 Another good way of raising baby spider plants is by putting small pots filled with compost next to the spider parent. Rest the baby on the pot and peg it down with a hairpin. After about ten days the little plant will have taken root. Now it will be strong enough to live on its own, so you can cut the stem joining it to its parent.

6 Put your plants in baskets and hang them up. Don't forget to water them, and soon they will have trailing leaves and runners to grow more plants from.

The Hanging Gardens of Babylon

The famous Hanging Gardens are one of the seven ancient Wonders of the World. The gardens no longer exist, but fortunately a Babylonian priest described them in all their glory. They were created over 2500 years ago by King Nebuchadnezzar II, when Babylon was the main city of ancient Mesopotamia. The city was situated on the Euphrates River, near modern Baghdad, the capital of Iraq. Some say that the king had the gardens built to delight his young bride and remind her of the Persian mountains from where she came. The king's workers built a series of brick terraces, complete with trees, shrubs, and flowers. Slaves pumped water from the river to the top of the terraces, so that it flowed down through channels and waterfalls. In the early 1900s, archaeologists claimed to have discovered remains of the Hanging Gardens among the buried ruins of Babylon.

Desert Plants

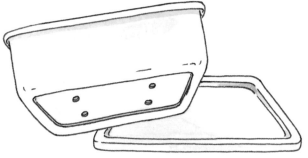

YOU WILL NEED:
- ✔ large plastic ice-cream container
- ✔ small pebbles ✔ cactus compost
- ✔ gardening gloves ✔ small stones
- ✔ selection of small cacti ✔ soap
- ✔ pieces of wood ✔ water
- ✔ charcoal (optional)

The main thing to remember about growing desert plants is that they need lots of sunshine and very little water. Cacti can live for several years in a spoonful of soil with only a few drops of water. You can buy lots of different types of cacti in garden centers. A good selection would be: *Opuntia* (prickly pear), *Rebutia, Echeveria, Echinocactus, Mammilaria,* and *Cephalocereus.*

1 Clean an empty ice-cream container with soap and water and let it dry completely. Ask an adult to pierce four holes in the bottom for drainage. You could use the lid as a tray to go underneath the container.

2 Cover the bottom of the container with a layer of small pebbles. You can also add some small pieces of charcoal to hold moisture and keep the soil sweet.

3 Fill the container up to two-thirds with sandy cactus compost.

4 Think about how you want to position your desert plants, and make one hole in the compost for each cactus. Wear gardening gloves to pick up your cacti, and handle them with great care. Cactus spines can be painful and difficult to remove if stuck in the skin.

Use a strip of paper to lift the cactus.

Cacti

There are around 2,000 different species of cacti, all of which are excellent examples of how plants can adapt to extreme conditions. Most cacti are desert plants, growing mainly in South and Central America, and in the American southwest. Mexico has the greatest variety of cacti.

The leaves or shoots of a cactus plant are spines, which help to protect it from desert animals. To prevent the loss of water, cacti have thick waxy outer layers, and water is stored in their spongy or hollow stems. The roots of cacti spread out close to the surface of the ground, so that they can quickly absorb water after any rainfall. One of the largest cacti, the saguaro, often grows to a height of 50 feet (15 meters). Many saguaros have holes in which woodpeckers and tiny desert owls live, safe from their enemies. The best known cacti are the prickly pears, so called because they bear a sweet, juicy fruit that looks like a pear.

5 Put the cacti in the holes and press the compost firmly around them. Complete your desert with interesting rock and wood shapes.

6 Water the cacti sparingly after planting. Then give them a little water every three weeks in summer, and every eight weeks in winter. Remember, cacti like a dry environment. One day they might surprise you with a beautiful show of flowers. If so, enjoy that special moment, because the flowers are short-lived. Some appear at night and are gone next morning.

Plants and Planting

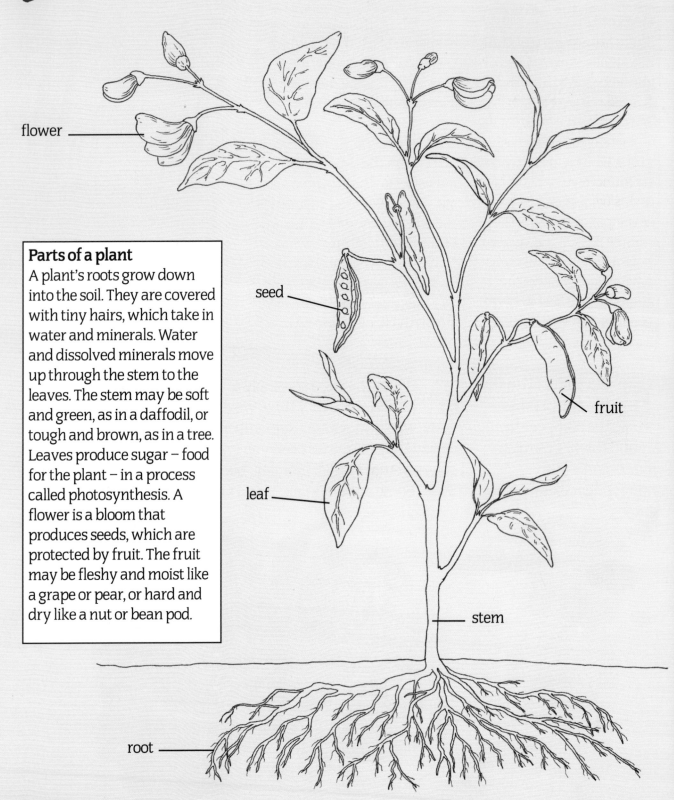

flower

seed

fruit

leaf

stem

root

Parts of a plant

A plant's roots grow down into the soil. They are covered with tiny hairs, which take in water and minerals. Water and dissolved minerals move up through the stem to the leaves. The stem may be soft and green, as in a daffodil, or tough and brown, as in a tree. Leaves produce sugar – food for the plant – in a process called photosynthesis. A flower is a bloom that produces seeds, which are protected by fruit. The fruit may be fleshy and moist like a grape or pear, or hard and dry like a nut or bean pod.

Parts of a flower

At the base of the flower are the leaflike sepals. Inside these are the brightly colored petals. Inside the petals are the stamens, or male parts of the flower, which are full of pollen grains. The stamens surround the pistil, or female part of the flower. At the base of the pistil is the ovary, which contains one or more ovules surrounding egg cells. When a pollen grain unites with an egg cell in the ovule, the ovule develops into a seed.

Some plants, such as a rose, contain both male and female parts in one flower. In other plants, such as holly, the male and female flowers are on separate plants. And in some plants, such as oak, the separate male and female flowers are on the same plant.

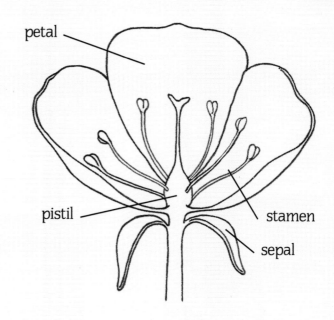

petal

pistil

stamen

sepal

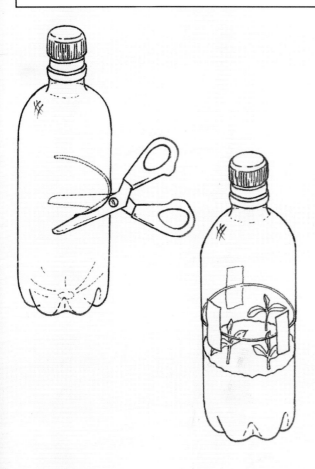

Planting seeds

Some seeds do not grow well if they are planted in an open garden. If you plant them indoors in spring, the seedlings will be big enough to plant in the garden when the weather is warm. You can make your own propagator. Cut around the middle of a plastic bottle, fill the bottom with compost, and scatter the seeds thinly. Just cover the seeds with compost and spray with water. Tape the top half back on the bottle and put it in a warm, dark place. Once the seedlings are large enough to handle, they can be put into seed trays. Plant them 2 inches (5 cm) apart, so they have room to grow. When the weather is warm enough, move the tray outside. When the seedlings are too big for the tray, dig small holes in the garden and plant them. Press the soil down and water.

Some good seeds to plant in this way are nasturtiums, snapdragons, and parsley.

Glossary

archaeologist – a scientist who studies the ancient past.

blight – a plant disease.

bud – a swelling on a plant stem containing leaves or flowers.

Buddhism – a religion founded in India in the sixth century B.C.

bulb – an underground storage organ for certain plants.

cactus (plural cacti) – a spiny desert plant.

chlorophyll – a green pigment in plants.

compost – any mixture of soil and decayed organic matter in which plants are grown, especially in pots.

dormant – alive but resting.

embryo – the part of a seed that develops into a plant.

fungus (plural fungi) – a very simple living thing, such as a mushroom.

gravel – a mixture of small pieces of rock.

ikebana – the Japanese art of flower arranging.

insectivorous – feeding on insects.

mildew – a fungus that causes disease in the leaves, stems, or fruit of green plants.

mold – a fungus that causes growth on food stored in damp conditions.

nutrient – a substance that gives life and growth.

oasis – a fertile patch in a desert.

ovary – the part of a flower that contains ovules which enclose the egg cells.

photosynthesis – the process used by plants to feed themselves, in which they use the energy from sunlight to turn water and gas into food.

pistil – the female part of a flower.

pitcher – a large jug; the pitcher plant has leaves shaped like this.

pod – a seed case, such as those that contain beans or peas.

pollen – grains that unite with egg cells in ovules to produce seeds.

prey – an animal hunted by another animal or a plant for food.

propagator – a heated box used to develop seeds.

protein – a substance that forms an essential part of all living things.

sap – a liquid that carries food to all parts of a plant.

seedling – a small plant produced from a seed.

sepal – part of the outer envelope that surrounds a flower bud.

shrub – a woody plant, smaller than a tree.

spore – a fungus cell that develops into a new growth.

stamen – the male part of a flower.

Resources

tropical – situated in the tropics, the hottest part of the earth's surface near the equator.

trowel – a small hand tool shaped like a spade, used for lifting plants.

twig – a small branch.

yeast – a fungus that turns sugar to carbon dioxide and alcohol.

Gardening by Mary Logue (Child's World 1992)

Gardening: A Kid's Guide to Messing Around in the Dirt by Kim G. Raferty and Kevin Raferty (Klutz Press, 1989)

Gardening Projects for Children by Tanya Bigge (Murdoch, 1992)

Green Thumbs Up! The Science of Growing Plants by Peter Bull (Random Books, 1992)

Grow It! An Indoor-Outdoor Gardening Guide for Kids by Erika Markmann (Random Books, 1991)

Grow It For Fun by Denny Robson (Gloucester Press, 1991)

Growing Plants by Barbara Taylor (Warwick, 1991)

Growing Things by Sean McCann (Dufour, 1989)

My First Garden Book by NK Lawn & Garden Company (Avon, 1986)

My First Nature Book by Angela Wilkes (Knopf, 1990)

Nature Detective: Plants by Anita Ganeri (Watts, 1991)

Plants by Anita Ganeri (Watts, 1992)

Index

Additional Photographs:

Bruce Coleman 7, 9, 17, 19, 23, 27; Mary Evans 25; Robert Harding 13, 15; Photos Horticultural 9; Zefa 4-5, 11, 21

DATE DUE			

11630

635.9   Morris, Ting.
MOR
        Growing things

WITHDRAWN

MCMULLEN BOOTH ELEMENTARY

835300 01496   31405B   004